ALOHA
· WAIKIKI ·

100 Years of Pictures
From Hawaii's Most Famous Beach
by DeSoto Brown

Editions Limited

Published by Editions Limited
1123 Kapahulu Avenue Honolulu, Hawaii 96816

Produced by David Rick
ISBN 0-9607938-9-5 (softcover)

Printed in Hong Kong
5 4 3 2 1 0

For information regarding this book, please contact the publisher. A special mahalo to Maryann Ferguson and Butch Cole, two friends who donated treasured possessions now seen in this book.

The fun-loving gals of Waikiki: an early 1960s postcard (**left**), the "bachelor girl" from 1942 and the "virgin" from 1928 (**above**), and movie star Betty Compson on the beach in 1934 (**right**).

Previous page: McKinley High School students in a publicity pose, 1931.

The World's Happiest Rendezvous

HAWAII'S WAIKIKI

Pronouncing the name "Waikiki" just naturally molds your lips in a smile. And that's as it should be. For the curve of a smile is the graceful crescent of her shore . . . its quick brightness, the sun playing on her velvet sands . . . its gaiety, the infectious mirth rippling among her colorful throng.

At night, it becomes a kind of Mona Lisa smile of tantalizing promise and mystery.

For those who seek novelty with their diversions and complete relaxation in a setting of exotic beauty, Waikiki is the world's happiest rendezvous.

Introduction

Waikiki: symbol of the tropical Pacific, with a reputation (like the flowery 1930s description on the facing page) that's known just about everywhere. Even those who might not know its name can recognize that almost too-famous view of Diamond Head and its nearby curve of sandy shoreline. Waikiki may not be *the* most famous beach in the world, but it's certainly one of them — and it's easily the best-known part of Hawaii.

But Waikiki is more than just a beach. It's actually an entire district that today is a crowded urban area; a city within a city whose population at peak periods is edging towards 100,000 people. Yet one hundred years ago Waikiki was an agricultural swampland, home to a handful of farmers and fishermen and a few well-to-do families with beach homes. You don't need to be a kamaaina to understand what tremendous changes have occurred to make this place what it now is.

Aloha Waikiki isn't meant to tell the entire story of this transformation, but it will provide a visual journey through Waikiki's period of greatest change. Much of this photographic journey will be a fresh one too, for although some of these historical pictures might be familiar, many have never appeared in print before, or have not been seen for years. Today we can admire the original photographers who were wise enough to chronicle the Waikiki environment of their time, and we can thank those people who continue to work with and preserve these valuable pictures, especially at the Hawaii State Archives and the Bishop Museum Photo Collection.

Probably you weren't here to watch all of Waikiki's evolution. If that's the case, then let *Aloha Waikiki* show you something of what you missed.

Queen's Surf

Private homes were almost the only thing along the shore when these two ladies meandered down Queen's Surf beach in 1886 (**facing page**). One hundred years later (**above**), multistory hotels are all you can see.

Canoe-surfing, Waikiki.

Left: pa'u riders gather in Kapiolani Park for some special occasion in the early years of the century. **Below,** another park scene — members of the kamaaina Judd family lounge on the bank of one of the area's large ponds during a picnic in the summer of 1890.

Left: narrow treadmarks of wagon wheels run parallel to streetcar tracks on the dirt road into Waikiki around 1900. The beach is straight ahead, hidden by the groves of kiawe trees and coconut palms.

Moana Hotel, Maikiki, Honolulu.

When it opened in 1901, the Moana Hotel was easily the biggest and most exciting thing in "Maikiki" (note misspelling on postcard at **left**). It attracted well dressed beachgoers (**right**) who guarded against the elements with hats, gloves, and even veils. **Below** is the Moana in its original configuration, with its famous pier and large dining room standing on pilings. The pier was removed in the early 1930s; the dining room lasted until about 1947. The water to the left of the beach that the three boys are standing on will probably seem confusing—it's the mouth of a stream that emptied into the ocean at this location until the Ala Wai Canal was dug in the early 1920s.

Canoes were a part of the Waikiki scene for both work and pleasure. At **left,** a lei-wearing crew poses with their craft, perhaps after a race. **Right:** canoes covered by palm branches and lauhala mats await their owners on Kuhio Beach in 1886. Yes, those are telephone poles in the background; phones had been in use in Honolulu for more than 6 years by that time. The cover of a 1910 song folio (**inset**) illustrates a similar scene.

Right: two men take their dogs along for a short afternoon trip in a sailing canoe from a private home on the coast near Diamond Head.

The Cocoa Palm
Songs for Children
by
Mary Dillingham Frear
Oliver Ditson Company

13

Waikiki's pleasantly sunny weather drew well-to-do residents to make their homes there. Most splendid of all these was "Kainalu" (**below**), built around 1900 by the Castle family. This immense structure, with its rooftop pavilion and tremendous rooms (**right**), was an area landmark for almost 60 years. For most of that time, however, it was the headquarters of the Elks Club, which is still located there today.

The Castles and their next door neighbors, the Hedemanns, enjoyed lovely days at Sans Souci Beach. At **right,** swimmers rest on a raft just offshore from those homes with Punchbowl Crater and palm-lined Waikiki Beach in the distance. Note that proper swimming attire in 1890 included hats!

Left and **below:** what 80 years of changes have brought to Kalakaua Avenue as it runs along Kuhio Beach, across from Kapiolani Park. The major difference, of course, is that the ocean no longer laps up against the low wall next to the street, for a wide area of manmade beach now exists there instead.

Left: much of Waikiki was still a semi-rural agricultural district in the beginning of the 20th century. This view of a lily pond and a fenced road, with banana groves across the street, is probably where the Royal Hawaiian Shopping Center on Kalakaua Avenue is today.

Kalakaua Avenue

Kalakaua Avenue was wide, unpaved, and uncrowded in 1915 (**facing page**). Seventy years later (**above**), thousands of vehicles pass this point every day.

Diamond Head, Honolulu.

Facing page: a palm-bordered drive in Kapiolani Park on an afternoon in 1912. **Above:** Waikiki was known for some time for its farms and duckponds. Here's a glimpse of the latter—with ducks—in 1919.

Although the pace of Waikiki was beginning to pick up a bit during the teen years, there were still private homes along the beach. One of the these belonged to the Hustace family, and it stood on the Diamond Head side of the Moana Hotel. The view at **left** shows the house as it looked from the Moana Pier about 1915, and **below** is the home with its well-kept front yard seen from Kalakaua Avenue. Above the front steps hangs a small sign that reads "Hustace Villa".

Left: members of the Hedemann family in their automobile at their Waikiki home, located at the Sans Souci area, photographed about 1911.

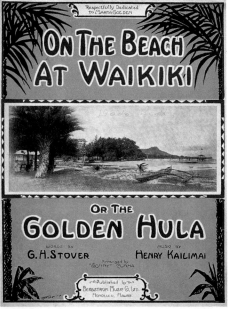

Popular music served to spread the fame of Waikiki all throughout the United States in the late teen years. "On The Beach At Waikiki", from 1915, (sheet music, **left**) was the first of such tunes to really make it big. The "sweet brown maiden" mentioned in the song, who "gave me language lessons on the beach at Waikiki" is nowhere to be seen in the photo **below,** taken in front of the Outrigger Canoe Club at the same period.

Another piece of sheet music (from 1916, **below**) shows a romantic couple who look quite similar to some real beachgoers of the same era (**left**).

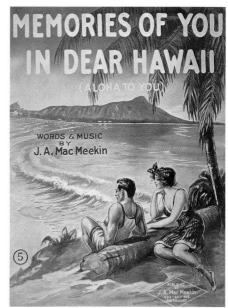

Early accommodations for Hawaii's small number of tourists included these beachside hotels. Cassidy's Cottages (**left**) stood where the Hawaiian Village Hotel is today and included this little pergola (**below**) where you could sit and gaze at Diamond Head, as the woman in the photo is doing. **Right:** five guests stand on the lawn of the Seaside Hotel, which during the next decade would be replaced by the Royal Hawaiian Hotel on this site. Just over the shoulder of the man on the left is the Castle home, illustrated on p. 14.

Left: Kalakaua Avenue stretches back towards Punchbowl Crater in 1915, with practically no sign of any traffic. That small beach community has now become a city unto itself — 70 years' difference between Kalakaua Avenue near the Kapahulu Avenue intersection in 1915 (**below**) and today (**right**).

Concrete Curb along Boulevard
Sept. 16 1924.

Ala Wai Boulevard

Ala Wai Boulevard was constructed on the newly-filled in land of Waikiki in 1924 (**facing page**).
Sixty years later (**above**), a multitude of buildings block the former view of Diamond Head.

The construction of the Ala Wai Canal between 1921 and 1924 altered Waikiki forever. The streams that had flowed all the way to the beach were now intercepted by the new waterway, and that meant the end of the swamps and ponds that had kept most of the district in agricultural use. Furthermore, the canal now formed a distinct boundary that separated Waikiki from the rest of Honolulu, which was a division that had been somewhat hazy in the past. **Left:** the Ala Wai with the first few houses of the "new" Waikiki off in the distance. **Above:** soldiers march informally down still-unpaved Ala Wai Boulevard with only 2 little boys and a dog to observe them.

Left: a Jazz Age miss poses on the running board of a new 1927 automobile near the Natatorium. Right: a quiet suburban-looking residential street is overshadowed by the new Royal Hawaiian Hotel in early 1927.

Right: the N. Aoki Market on Kalakaua Avenue across from Kuhio Beach sold the usual array of groceries and dispensed gasoline as well from its curbside pump. The store remained (although in a different building) in this location near Ohua Avenue until 1970.

The smart Winter Throng is gathering at **WAIKIKI**

Left: young surfers line up with their weighty wooden boards on the beach in front of the Outrigger Canoe Club. As demonstrated here, both sexes still wore one piece woolen bathing suits in the 1920s. **Inset:** a small decorative motif from a promotional brochure. **Above:** "The smart Winter Throng" takes to the water in a 1928 Hawaii Tourist Bureau advertisement.

Below: the Crabbe brothers, champion local swimmers, pose on the sands in front of the Royal Hawaiian Hotel. Buster Crabbe, on the right, was a 1932 Olympic gold medalist before he blasted off to a Hollywood career as outer space explorers Buck Rogers and Flash Gordon.

Luxurious and quite elegant was Waikiki's Royal Hawaiian Hotel, opened in 1927 and destined to become the queen of the beachside hostelries for decades to come. The brochure **above** announced its arrival, and soon wealthy guests like Hollywood stars Gilbert Roland and Norma Talmadge (**right**) were discovering the Royal's attractions.

Guests take afternoon tea in the Royal Hawaiian's colonnaded front hall overlooking the sea **(below)**. The waitresses are clad in Japanese kimonos, considered a quaint sort of uniform to wear until World War II brought Japanese culture into sudden disfavor.

Here's the menu that these happy people got to choose from **(above)**, offering everything from Tea Buns to Coco Hon-ee Toast, and all at quite reasonable prices.

Left: the Royal Hawaiian and Moana Hotels dominate their surroundings in this 1929 aerial view. Travelers were often disappointed by the very skimpy amount of sand at Waikiki in those days; look up past the Moana to see why. This stretch of beach has been considerably widened since then.

Above: the main entrance to the Royal Hawaiian Hotel off Kalakaua Avenue looked like a simple driveway through some lush gardens in 1927. Today, 60 years later, the Royal Hawaiian Shopping Center sits in the same spot (**left**). The entry road was moved to its present location, opposite Royal Hawaiian Avenue, when the center was constructed around 1980.

Ala Wai Canal

The Ala Wai Canal was lined with buildings no taller than these young palm trees in 1937 (**facing page**). Fifty years later (**above**), those same palm trees have grown—but so have the buildings.

The silver surf of Waikiki

Here are the delights of "the silver surf of Waikiki" during the 1930s. Surfers await waves (**facing page**), while beachboys Sally Hale and Sam Colgate prepare to take radio songstress Ruth Etting for a canoe ride (**below left**). Illustrations from promotional literature carry on the watery theme (**left** and **below right**).

Left: champion surfer Tom Blake and 3 female friends pause for a refreshing drink of coconut milk, and at **right,** starlet Florence Rice finds that just about anything is yours for the asking at Waikiki, even a telephone! Both photographs were intended for promotional use to help publicize the islands.

Right: an artistic vision of Waikiki's aquatic activities from a 1931 Hawaii Tourist Bureau advertisement.

HAWAII

548 Waikiki Theater - Honolulu, Hawaii

The swankiest moviehouse in the islands was the Waikiki Theater, which opened in 1936. **Left** is a postcard view of its facade as seen from Kalakaua Avenue, showing the gardens and front courtyard. **Below,** the Waikiki's usherettes line up for inspection from their costumed leader, whose function it was to stand in the lobby and direct patrons to the right or left aisle of the auditorium.

Transportation to the beach could take different forms. **Below:** those who could afford it might choose to travel in a new 1935 Chevrolet, here being shown with the famous coastline in the background. A more economical way to get to Waikiki was via a "swift gliding Trolley Coach" of the Honolulu Rapid Transit Company, as illustrated in the 1939 ad shown at **right.**

You're headed for "Fun" at Waikiki!

All aboard for a care-free day at the beach . . . daddy, mother and the youngsters, sand pails and all. Away on a swift gliding Trolley Coach for a Waikiki adventure.

No matter where you wish to go in Honolulu, or what you wish to see and do, you'll find HRT city-wide service at your command.

HONOLULU RAPID TRANSIT COMPANY, LTD.

The Halekulani Hotel was a low-key sort of place whose tranquility appealed to an upper crust clientele. At **left** is its charming lobby; **above** is a bookplate designed by famous local artist Juliette May Fraser and used in the hotel's library. A chauffered Rolls-Royce waits at the front entrance in 1935 (**right**).

"Hawaii's Beach Hotels" were the subject of the brochure **above.** Featured on the cover was the Royal Hawaiian, which celebrated its 8th birthday on February 6, 1935 with this novel cake (**right**). The chef will have to cut carefully around those live hula girls adorning the confection!

Left: wicker furniture brings a touch of informality to a corner of the lanai of the suite illustrated below.

Right: a room plan from the late 1930s shows one type of accommodation available at the Royal Hawaiian. The daily rates quoted were not inexpensive for that time. Still, this was not by any means the most deluxe sort of suite you could get there.

16
Queen Liliuokalani Suites
Kuhio Suites

Consisting of two double bedrooms, each with twin beds, private tub bath with shower, sitting room and screened lanai.

- Overlooking the gardens.
- Available on mezzanine, first and second floors.

DAILY RATES
American Plan

QUEEN LILIUOKALANI SUITES		KUHIO SUITES	
Entire suite, 1 or 2 persons	$56	Entire suite, 1 or 2 persons	$43
3 persons	$66	3 persons	$53
4 persons	$76	4 persons	$63
Part of suite, consisting of one double bedroom, private tub bath with shower, sitting room and screened lanai.		*Part of suite, consisting of one double bedroom, private tub bath with shower, sitting room and screened lanai.*	
1 person	$38	1 person	$29
2 persons	$48	2 persons	$39

ROYAL HAWAIIAN HOTEL

Not all of Waikiki was glamorous. Taking care of everyday needs were places like the Beach Clothes Cleaner (**facing page**), and the Waikiki Market (**left,** and a matchbook cover **lower left**). Today, 50 years later, the now-unoccupied building still stands at the corner of Kalakaua Avenue and Ena Road (**below**).

WAIKIKI MARKET
LIQUOR DEPT.
phone 91932

Kalakaua Avenue

Kalakaua Avenue was unhurried at the end of World War II in 1945 (**facing page**). Forty years later (**above**), the only thing that seems unchanged is the huge banyan tree across the street.

Left: wearing their best shoes, these visitors strolled through the wet sand in front of the Royal Hawaiian around 1940. With the shocking arrival of World War II in 1941, barbed wire soon disfigured this same spot (**below**) as well as others down the beach (**right**).

Thinking of a place in Waikiki?

Above: if you were "thinking of a place in Waikiki" (as suggested **above** by Reddy Kilowatt of the Hawaiian Electric Company), then perhaps the bargain at **right,** advertised in 1942, would appeal to you. Sorry, the price is no longer in effect! **Facing page:** the view up one of Waikiki's side streets in the early 1940s suggests a quiet, well-kept suburb.

BUY TODAY

Now is the time to live in your own home.
Here are a few homes for your selection

IN THE HEART OF WAIKIKI

Yet it has all the privacy of a country home. This well built home designed by one of Honolulu's leading architects is only 5 years old. The large living room, sun porch and dining room have hardwood floors. There are 3 large bedrooms, modern bathroom with extra lavatory and toilet adjoining one bedroom. Large modern kitchen with tile sink and plenty of cupboards, etc. Separate garage and laundry room. The lot area has over 7,500 sq. ft. with a nice lawn, shrubs and trees.

$9,500

Nighttime Waikiki offered many entertainments. The Kuhio Theater (**left**) was almost ready to open in 1941, but ended up as a storage facility for Naval records all during the war years and didn't begin to show films until June 1945. Lau Yee Chai (**above**), located at 2020 Kuhio avenue, billed itself as "the world's most beautiful Chinese restaurant". Its menu (**upper right**) boasted over 100 selections, and every night you could enjoy "the acme in entertainment and relaxation" in its back gardens (**right**).

Here's how the beach looked to some photographers and artists in the 1940s. **Below:** posed models demonstrate just about everything you ever thought you'd see at Waikiki, and at **right,** a dapper fellow from a 1946 advertisement shows off the stylish clothes he got at Klein's Store for Men in Honolulu. **Facing page:** this cartoon on the cover of the Outrigger Canoe Club's menu names favorite surfing spots and illustrates seaside activities from a lomilomi massage to a pale tourist struggling in the "malihini surf".

Far left: a postcard of the Moana Hotel's main building as seen from across Kalakaua Avenue at the Moana Cottages, and **near left,** the cover of a hotel matchbook.

Right: the weekly broadcast of the "Hawaii Calls" radio show, being heard all over the country, draws a crowd to the Moana Hotel's Banyan Court.

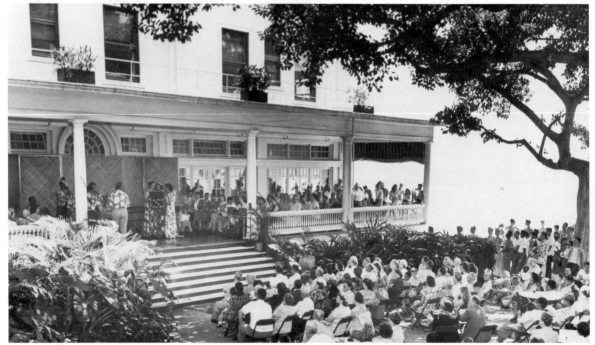

Near right: a Royal Hawaiian Hotel matchbook, and **far right,** an artistic postcard view of the Royal seen from offshore with some topographically incorrect mountains behind it.

Left: visitors sip cocktails on the oceanside terrace of the Royal Hawaiian. The hotel spent World War II as a Navy rest center and did not reopen until extensive renovations were completed in 1946.

Left: a gas station and drugstore give Waikiki the look of Anytown, U.S.A. in 1945. The view is looking ewa from the intersection of Kalakaua Avenue and Uluniu Street; down the road a bit is the Moana Hotel.

Right: a lei woman strings flowers at the back of her truck parked in front of the Royal Hawaiian Hotel's gardens on Kalakaua Avenue in 1946. Selling leis on Waikiki's main street like this went on until the early 1960s.

Left: before Kewalo Basin became the port for most local fishing boats, many anchored along the Ala Wai Canal, as seen in this 1945 photograph. Forty years ago, the same Hobron Lane area that's now so crowded was almost deserted.

Right: as seen from the Ala Wai Bridge today, the Hobron Lane district (on the far side of the Ala Wai Canal) is a jungle of highrises with nearly the highest population density in Hawaii.

From Diamond Head

From the top of Diamond Head, Waikiki looked remarkably undeveloped in 1958 (**facing page**). Thirty years later (**above**), the open space of Kapiolani Park contrasts sharply with the built-up district that now exists.

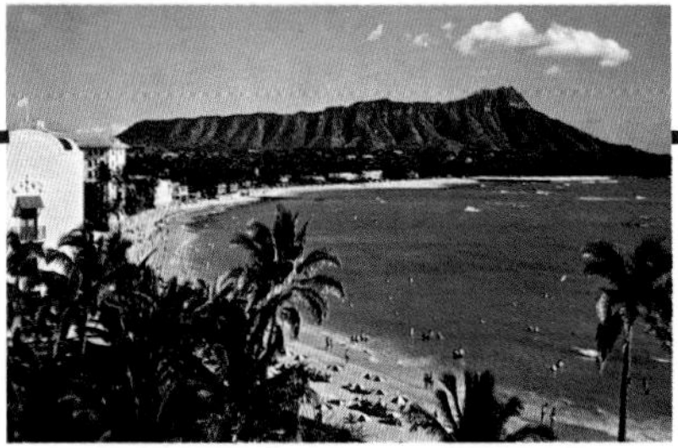

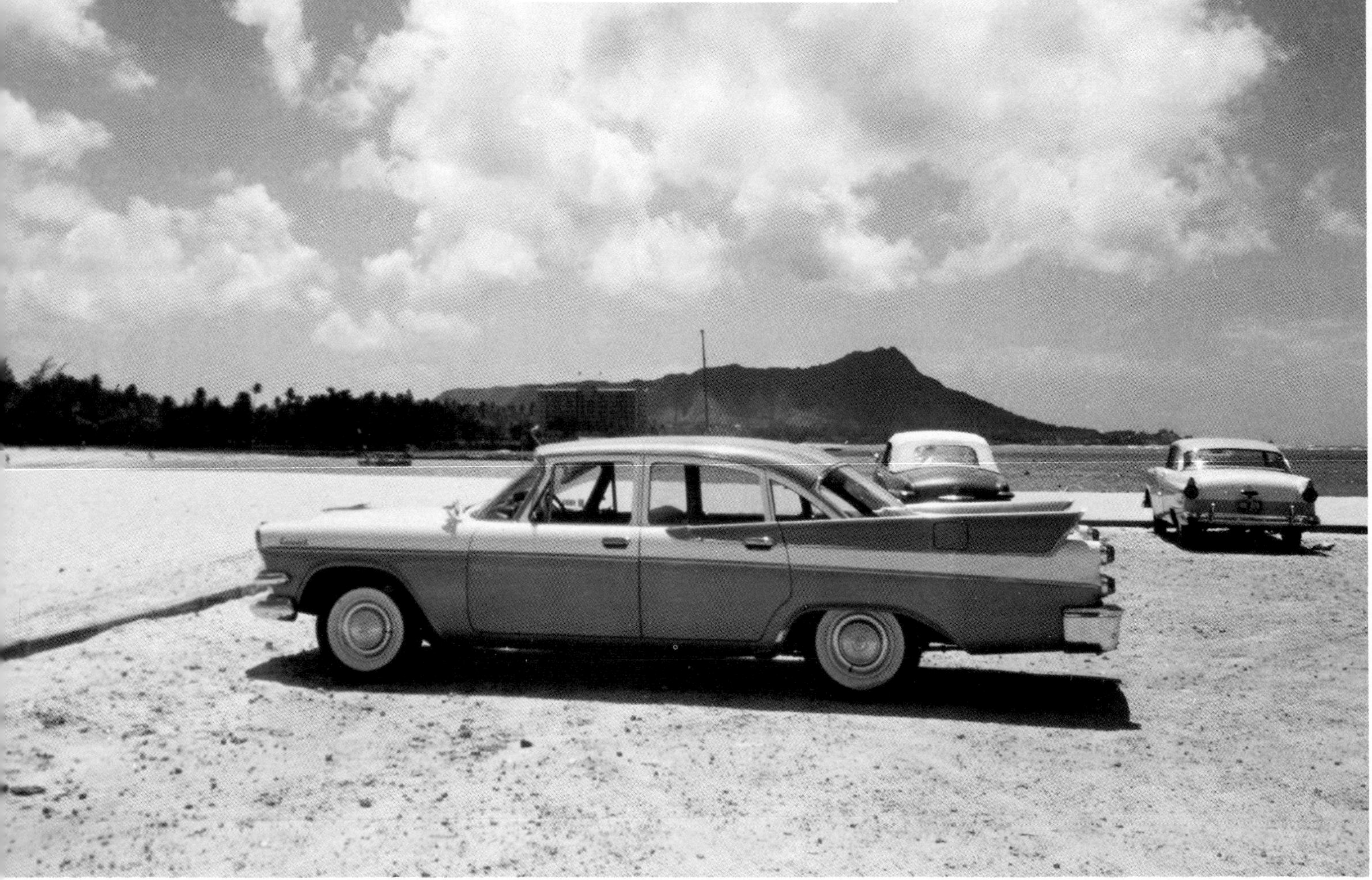

Left: the recently-developed beach coastline fronting the Kaiser Hawaiian Village Hotel provides a parking area for a brand new 1957 Dodge. **Above:** by the mid 1950s, hotels of a relatively modest 10 stories or so had started to appear above the palm groves, bringing a new and more active atmosphere to Waikiki. Among the innovations: swimming pools, like the one at **right** at the Reef Hotel, which meant that you didn't even have to go to the beach to get wet.

What better souvenir for the visitor than something you could wear? The girl at **left,** seated at a curbside lei wagon, offers a hat adorned with small Hawaiian novelties like a paper hibiscus flower and and a net filled with shells. **Above,** a similar pair of straw hats strolls down Kalakaua Avenue near Olohana Street in 1959.

Wearable souvenirs for men included the matching aloha-print bathing suit and shirt combo sometimes known as a "cabana set" (**above**), which was enthusiastically received in the 1950s. By today's standards, $12.50 for a silk shirt like the one "Seen at the Royal" (**right**) is a bargain we'll never see again.

Seen at the Royal

Pure silk aloha shirt— light as a passing breeze— hand-screened with an unusual new shell pattern. Short sleeves, 12.50 Long sleeves, 15.00

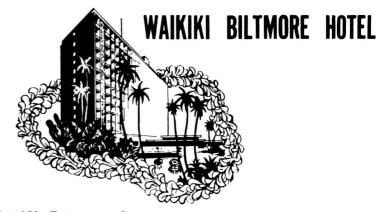

WAIKIKI BILTMORE HOTEL

Waikiki was growing in the 1950s. **Facing page:** the construction of the Surfrider Hotel at the beginning of the decade eventually eliminated this view of Diamond Head from the top of the Moana Hotel. (The site it was built on is the same as the Hustace home, seen on p. 23). Another major hotel of the fifties was the Biltmore (**left**), which unsuccessfully tried to be fashionable with features like a rooftop nightclub that never quite caught on. The most excitement the Biltmore managed to generate was when it was demolished in 1974 (**below**) to make room for the Hyatt Regency Hotel.

Waikiki's Biggest Show of the Year

HAVE **FUN**
ON WAIKIKI BEACH

A group of boys clowns for the camera and shows how to "have FUN on Waikiki Beach" (**inset,** from a 1954 surfboard rental company ad).

Beachgoers frolic in the wash of a wave in front of the Outrigger Canoe Club around 1955. The promotional stamp (**inset**) dates from the same period.

EVERY DAY OF THE YEAR

ON THE BEACH AT WAIKIKI

Left: from the 1950s through the 1970s, you could rent a little boat like this one for a scenic cruise on the Ala Wai Canal (seen here in about 1953). **Facing page, right:** what 30 years of changes have brought to the same vista, taken from next to the McCully Street Bridge where the boat rental stand once operated.

Above: a panoramic view from the end of the Kapahulu Groin, photographed about 1953, shows a lowrise Waikiki still awaiting the appearance of most of today's structures. The Royal Hawaiian and Moana/Surfrider Hotels are visible at the left, while Kalakaua Avenue facing Kuhio Beach is lined with one-story restaurants and stores. The Aoki Market, pictured on p. 34 (but now housed in a newer building), is located at the center of the panorama.

"Here's Waikiki"

An Aerial View

Waikiki was growing fast when this postcard was printed in 1965 (**facing page**). Twenty years later (**above**), that skyward growth has reached a level that probably can't go much farther—or can it?

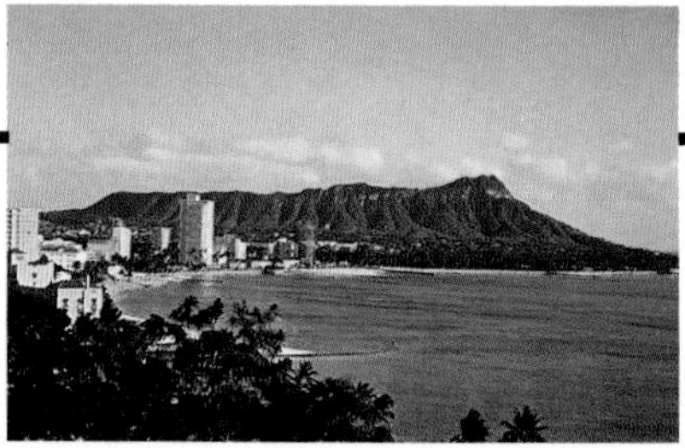

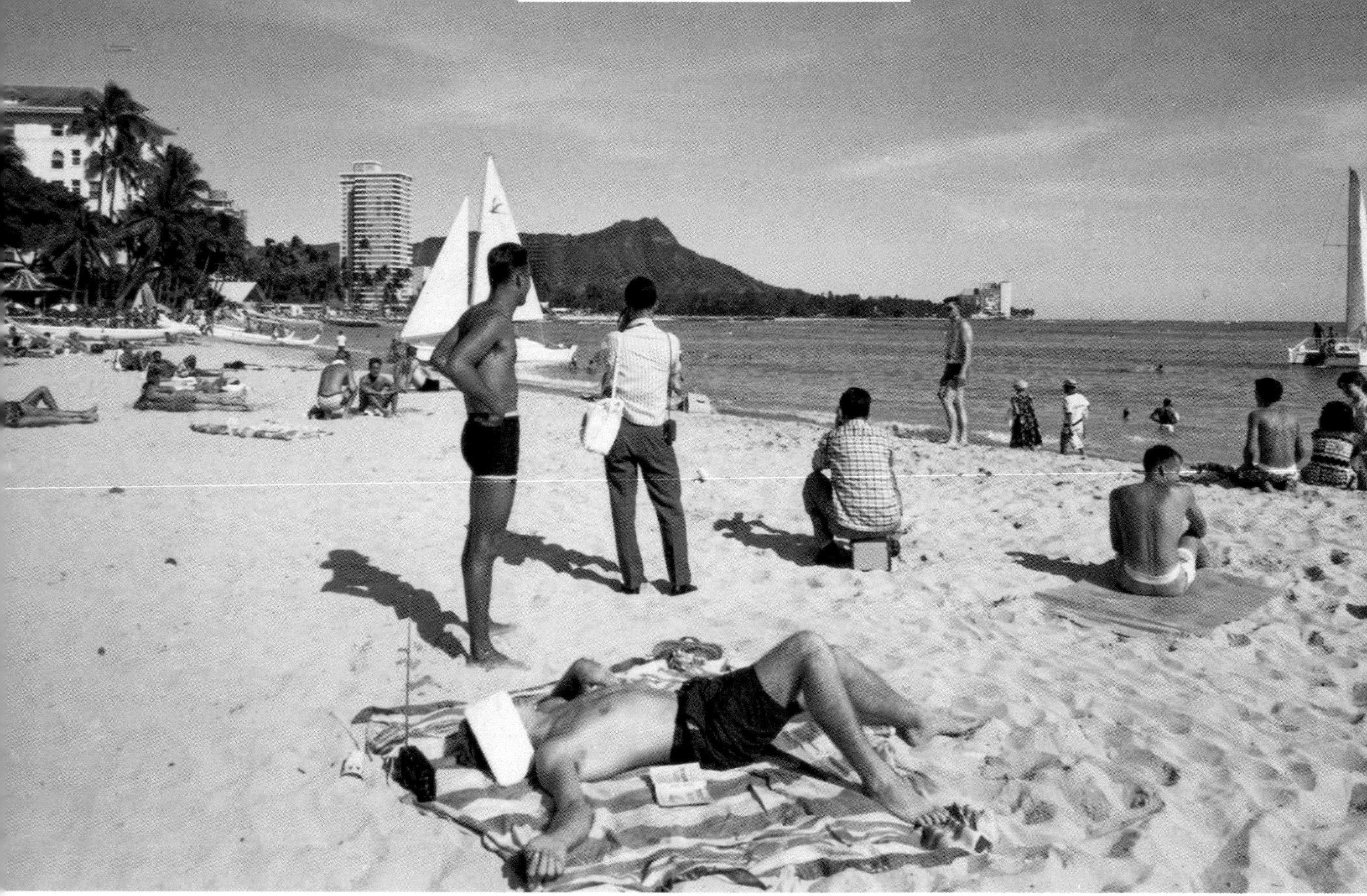

Canoes at Waikiki were mainly used for recreational purposes. **Below:** two beachboys prepare to take a wedged-in, happy bunch of tourists out to ride the waves, while at **left** a canoe serves an equally popular role as a prop for a pretty girl in a sixties postcard.

Left: visitors enjoyed the beach as they always had, but there were changes in the Waikiki of the 1960s. Just to the left of the sailboat in this photo is the 25 story Foster Tower, the first of Waikiki's really tall buildings. Farther off in the distance, near the base of Diamond Head, another cluster of highrises stands where the huge Castle home (p. 14) once dominated the surroundings.

Tourism increased dramatically in the 1960s, spurred by inexpensive jet travel (and airline brochures like the one **above**). Dealing with all these new travelers meant more planning and less spontaneity (**right**), but the aloha spirit remained, as seen at the Kodak Hula Show in 1961 (**facing page**)

Left: a telephoto lens compresses the bustle of Waikiki's main street into a welter of signs and vehicles in 1967; the scene is the mauka side of Kalakaua Avenue looking towards the Kalaimoku Street intersection. **Above** is a similar view further down the street. At **right** the marquee of the Merry Monarch nightclub touts a typically sixties activity: "Nitely Au Go Go Dancing".

Right: Waikiki continued to attract the famous. John Lennon and George Harrison found that Beatlemania had spread just as hysterically to Hawaii as anywhere else when they stopped off in May 1964.

Tourists from the orient began to appear in greater numbers in Waikiki in the 1960s, but the real boom for them would not come until the next decade. Two early visitors were film director Satoru Takeuchi and his lovely wife, actress Fujiko Yamamoto (**above**), seen here strolling outside the Royal Hawaiian Hotel in 1962. **Right:** fashionable stripes mark this couple's vacation outfits.

Left: cars and a city bus plow slowly through a Kalakaua Avenue flood in 1965. Even though Waikiki had been drained 40 years before, the waters could still return to their old haunts if the rain fell heavily enough. **Below:** the intersection of Ala Moana Boulevard and Hobron Lane was busy in 1961, but the same view 20 years later (**right**), dominated by highrises like the Discovery Bay condominium, is far busier.

H - 51 Sunset Waikiki Beach - Honolulu

Regardless of whatever else has changed in Waikiki's last century, some things will remain as they always were — the sunset, and the moon over Diamond Head. **Left:** dusk at Kuhio Beach about 1955, **above:** a 1930s handtinted postcard, **upper right:** a 1920s promotional stamp, and **right:** an early 1960s postcard.

Photo Credits

Author's collection: 75 (left), 91.

Honolulu Star-Bulletin, John Titchen: 77 (below, all three). Reprinted with permission.

Hawaii State Archives: 3, 9 (below), 18, 24 (below), 28, 29 (below), 35, 36 (larger), 38 (right), 39 (left), 40, 41 (above), 42, 44 (larger), 45 (lower left), 46 (above), 47, 48 (below), 49 (below), 51 (right), 52 (right), 53 (left), 54, 58 (both), 61, 66 (below), 68 (below).

Bishop Museum Photo Collection: 8 (larger), 11 (below), 16, 20 (larger), 21, 30, 34 (below), 37 (right), 76.

Ray Jerome Baker:	1, 25 (above), 27, 32 (larger), 33, 55 (above), 56, 59, 62, 68 (above), 69 (above), 93 (left).
Robert Bonine:	11 (above), 25 (below).
Robert Edgeworth:	23 (both).
Alonzo Gartley:	9 (above), 12 (above).
Laurence Hata:	63 (upper left), 70, 72 (larger), 74 (both), 78 (larger), 79 (larger), 80 (below), 80–81, 84 (larger), 85 (right), 86 (right), 87, 88, 89 (both), 90 (both), 92, 94, 96.
C. J. Hedemann:	12 (below), 14 (both), 15, 17 (above), 22.
Henry Hill:	34 (above).
Tai Sing Loo:	67 (below), 73 (above).
A. Mitchell:	6, 13 (larger).